SCHOLASTIC

writing guide

With interactive resources on CD-ROM

C000001248

Adventure Stories

for ages
5-7

Sarah Snashall
and
Huw Thomas

Credits

Authors
Sarah Snashall and
Huw Thomas

Development Editor
Marion Archer

Editor
Margaret Eaton

Assistant Editor
Sarah Sodhi

Series Designer
Anna Oliwa

Designers
Paul Stockmans and
Liz Gilbert

Cover Illustration
Mark Oliver

Illustrations
Martha Hardy

CD-ROM Development
CD-ROM developed in
association with Infuze Ltd

Mixed Sources
Product group from well-managed
forests and other controlled sources
www.fsc.org Cert no. TT-COC-002769
© 1996 Forest Stewardship Council
FSC

Text © 2003, 2010 Sarah Snashall and Huw Thomas
© 2010 Scholastic Ltd

Designed using Adobe InDesign

Published by Scholastic Ltd,
Book End
Range Road
Witney
Oxfordshire
OX29 0YD
www.scholastic.co.uk

Printed by Bell & Bain

1 2 3 4 5 6 7 8 9   0 1 2 3 4 5 6 7 8 9

British Library Cataloguing-in-Publication Data
A catalogue record for this book is available from the British Library.

ISBN 978-1407-11249-7

The rights of Sarah Snashall and Huw Thomas to be identified as the authors of
this work have been asserted by them in accordance with the Copyright, Designs
and Patents Act 1988.
Extracts from the Primary National Strategy's Primary Framework for Literacy
(2006) www.standards.dfes.gov.uk/primaryframework © Crown copyright.
Reproduced under the terms of the Click Use Licence.

Acknowledgments
The publishers gratefully acknowledge permission to reproduce the following
copyright material: **Macmillan Children's Books** for the use of an extract and
illustrations from *The Giant Postman* by Sally Grindley and Wendy Smith. Text ©
2000 Sally Grindley; Illustrations © 2000 Wendy Smith (2000, Kingfisher);
Walker Books for the use of *Jolly Roger and the Pirates of Abdul the Skinhead* by
Colin McNaughton © 1998, Colin McNaughton (1988, Walker Books).
Every effort has been made to trace copyright holders for the works reproduced
in this book, and the publisher apologises for any inadvertent omissions.

CD-ROM Minimum specifications:

Windows 2000/XP/Vista	Mac OSX 10.4	
Processor: 1 GHz	RAM: 512 MB	Graphics card: 32bit
Audio card: Yes	CD-ROM drive speed: 8x	Hard disk space: 200MB
Screen resolution: 800x600		RM CC3

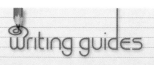

Contents

Introduction: Adventure Stories

The *Writing Guides* series aims to inspire and motivate children as writers by using creative approaches. Each *Writing Guide* contains activities and photocopiable resources designed to develop children's understanding of a particular genre (for example, fairy stories). The activities are in line with the requirements of the National Curriculum and the recommendations in the *Primary Framework for Literacy*. The teacher resource books are accompanied by a CD-ROM containing a range of interactive activities and resources.

What's in the book?

The *Writing Guides* series provides a structured approach to developing children's writing. Each book is divided into four sections.

Section 1: **Using good examples**
Three text extracts are provided to explore the typical features of the genre.

Section 2: **Developing writing**
There are ten short, focussed writing tasks in this section. These are designed to develop children's ability to use the key features of the genre in their own writing. The teachers' notes explain the objective of each activity and provide guidance on delivery, including how to use the photocopiable pages and the materials on the CD-ROM.

Section 3: **Writing**
The three writing projects in this section require the children to produce an extended piece of writing using the key features of the genre.

Section 4: **Review**
This section consists of a 'Self review', 'Peer review' and 'Teacher review'. These can be used to evaluate how effectively the children have met the writing criteria for the genre.

What's on the CD-ROM?

The accompanying CD-ROM contains a range of motivating activities and resources. The activities can be used for independent work or can be used on an interactive whiteboard to enhance group teaching.
Each CD-ROM contains:
- three text extracts that illustrate the typical features of the genre
- interactive versions of selected photocopiable pages
- four photographs and an audio file to create imaginative contexts for writing
- a selection of writing templates and images which can be used to produce extended pieces of writing.

The interactive activities on the CD-ROM promote active learning and support a range of teaching approaches and learning styles. For example, drag and drop and sequencing activities will support kinaesthetic learners.

Talk for writing

Each *Writing Guide* uses the principles of 'Talk for writing' to support children's writing development by providing opportunities for them to rehearse ideas orally in preparation for writing. 'Talk for writing' is promoted using a variety of teaching strategies including discussions, questioning and drama activities (such as, developing imaginative dialogue – see *Fantasy Stories for Ages 9–11*).

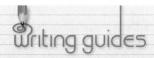

How to use the CD-ROM

Start screen: click on the 'Start' button to go to the main menu.

This section contains brief instructions on how to use the CD-ROM. For more detailed guidance, go to 'How to use the CD-ROM' on the start screen or click on the 'Help' button located in the top right-hand corner of the screen.

Installing the CD-ROM

Follow the instructions on the disk to install the CD-ROM onto your computer. Once the CD-ROM is installed, navigate to the program location and double click on the program icon to open it.

Main menu screen

Main menu

The main menu provides links to all of the writing activities and resources on the CD-ROM. Clicking on a button from the main menu will take you to a sub-menu that lists all of the activities and resources in that section. From here you have the option to 'Launch' the interactive activities, which may contain more than one screen, or print out the activities for pupils to complete by hand.

If you wish to return to a previous menu, click the 'Menu' button in the top right-hand corner of the screen; this acts as a 'back' button.

Screen tools

A range of simple writing tools that can be used in all of the writing activities are contained in the toolbar at the bottom of the screen.

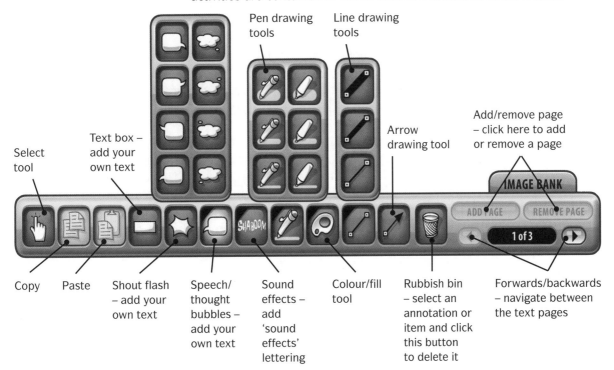

Pen drawing tools

Line drawing tools

Select tool

Text box – add your own text

Arrow drawing tool

Add/remove page – click here to add or remove a page

Copy

Paste

Shout flash – add your own text

Speech/ thought bubbles – add your own text

Sound effects – add 'sound effects' lettering

Colour/fill tool

Rubbish bin – select an annotation or item and click this button to delete it

Forwards/backwards – navigate between the text pages

Print

Save your work to chosen files

Open – navigate to your saved file to open your previous work

Reset the page

Printing and saving work

All of the resources on the CD-ROM are printable. You can also save and retrieve any annotations made on the writing activities. Click on the 'Controls' tab on the right-hand side of the screen to access the 'Print', 'Open', 'Save' and 'Reset screen' buttons.

View all thumbnails by clicking on the arrows

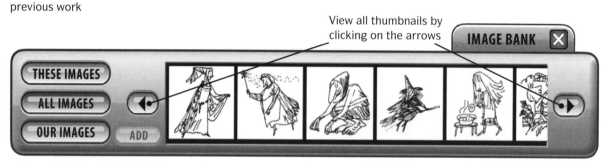

Image bank – click and drag an image to add it to an activity

Image bank

Each CD-ROM has an 'Image bank' containing images appropriate to the genre being taught. Click on the tab at the bottom right of the screen to open the 'Image bank'. On the left-hand side there are three large buttons.

- The 'These images' button will display only the images associated with the specific activity currently open.
- The 'All images' button will display all the photographs and illustrations available on the CD-ROM.
- The 'Our images' button will contain any images you or the children have added to the CD-ROM.

Press the left or right arrows to scroll through the images available. Select an image and drag and drop it into the desired location on the screen. If necessary, resize the image using the arrow icon that appears at the bottom right of the image.

You can upload images to the 'Image bank', including digital photographs or images drawn and scanned into the computer. Click on 'Our images' and then 'Add' to navigate to where the image is stored. A thumbnail picture will be added to the gallery.

Writing your own story

Each CD-ROM contains a selection of blank writing templates. The fiction genre templates will be categorised under the button 'My story' and the non-fiction templates will be categorised under 'My recount' or 'My writing'. The writing templates encourage the children to produce an extended piece of genre writing. They can also add images, speech bubbles and use other tools to enhance their work.

The fiction titles also include a cover template for the children to use. They can customise their cover by adding their own title, blurb and images.

Section 1

Using good examples

Using adventure stories

Adventure stories are a clear and enjoyable genre for children. They are typically structured around a hero who goes on a journey with a goal and encounters villains and other dangers on the way. The action-led plots, combined with uncomplicated 'good' and 'bad' characters, can be simple for the children to read, enjoy and plan for themselves. There's also something about the spirit of adventure that children need to feel: that continuous arc of danger and safety that characters travel through as they engage in their quest.

When reading adventure stories, children can draw on their own experience of such stories from books they have read, or from films and television programmes, and can use this knowledge to inform their thinking about their own adventure stories.

Types of adventure stories

The text extracts on photocopiable pages 10, 11 and 12 cover three different starting points for adventure stories: a kidnap (*Jolly Roger*); a danger that arrives in a safe setting (the ordinary village that is disrupted by a visitor from outside in *The Giant Postman*); and a challenge that will lead to a dangerous quest (the discovery of a note in *Skull Island*, which will lead to a rescue attempt).

As each story begins, we do not know what dangers may lie ahead for our three main characters. Danger is a key feature in adventure stories: a villain who must be evaded, a dangerous intruder in an everyday setting, or a dangerous setting that must be navigated through, avoiding such obstacles as creatures living in woods or rocky mountains.

Links to the Primary Framework

With the opportunity to create well-developed characters, exciting action and unexpected events, adventure stories also allow children to exercise their imagination. In Year 1, adventure stories could be the basis for working on Literacy Framework Unit 4, 'Stories about fantasy worlds'.

At Key Stage 1, children need to be able to progress from single-line stories to the beginnings of paragraph writing, where an event can be developed. Adventure stories provide good opportunities to explore Literacy Framework Year 2 Unit 4 'Extended stories', as they unfold a storyline that has a goal, often going through a series of stages and problems.

Adventure story features

Characters
- Heroes who respond to a challenge.
- Villains to oppose the hero.

Settings
- Dangerous settings providing a range of challenges for the hero.
- Dangers in settings become part of the plot.

Plot
- A quest structure.
- Series of triumphs and setbacks.

Language features
- Descriptive depiction of settings.
- Insights into what a character is feeling.

Section 1: Using good examples

Extract 1: Jolly Roger

What's on the CD-ROM

Jolly Roger
- Text extract to read and discuss.

Oh no!
- Drag and drop story events into the correct order.
- Type in further ideas to embellish the plot.

This humorous version of the classic 'kidnapped by pirates' tale contains all the classic adventure elements: a hero, villains, a dangerous setting, something to search for (Roger's dad) and lots of great vocabulary.

- Open the extract on the CD-ROM and read it with drama. What adventure story features can the children spot? Who is the hero? How do they know? Do they want to know what happens next? Emphasise the fact that suspense is a key element of adventure stories.

- What about the villains? Ask: *What do you think the pirates are like?* Underline words that show how evil and foul they are (such as 'oozed and slithered'). Ask the children to read out their favourite sentences.

- Organise the children to carry out the activity 'Oh no!' from the CD-ROM or on photocopiable page 13. As they order the statements, ask them to consider: *What might Roger be thinking here?* Ask them to make notes on what else could have happened at each point.

- In Colin McNaughton's book *Jolly Roger and the Pirates of Abdul the Skinhead* (from which the text extract is taken), the pirate ship never leaves the harbour and the pirates turn out to be not very evil at all. Invite the children to consider what might happen next.

Extract 2: The Giant Postman

What's on the CD-ROM

The Giant Postman
- Text extract to read and discuss.

What they thought
- Drag and drop the thoughts of each character into the correct thought bubble.

This extract provides another common adventure story set up: a community is threatened, so someone goes on a quest to stop the danger.

- Open the text extract on the CD-ROM. Point out that the hero of the story is one of the youngest members of the community. Highlight how the author shows Billy's bravery: 'The crowd gasped'.

- Ask: *Is there a villain here? Is there any 'villain' vocabulary?* (No, rather than a villain, we have a character who creates danger. Rather than a dangerous setting we have an everyday setting that has been made dangerous by an intruder.) Ask: *What else might threaten an everyday setting?* (A shark or an alien, for example.)

- Provide pairs of children with photocopiable page 14 'What they thought'. Ask them to discuss what the characters felt and to fill in the thought bubbles, making reference to the passage. If you are using the CD-ROM version, ask the children to drag and drop the thoughts of each character into the appropriate thought bubbles.

- At the end of the passage, Billy resolves to visit the postman. Ask: *What does this tell us about him? What might the other characters say about Billy?* Can the children see that this makes Billy a hero? Encourage them to discuss what will happen next in the story. What will Billy encounter in the Giant Postman's house? You might want to introduce the idea that the postman might be friendly (as he turns out to be). Encourage them to consider this variation on the storyline.

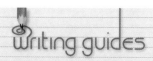

Extract 3: Skull Island

What's on the CD-ROM

Skull Island
- Text extract to read, discuss and edit.

The text extract 'Skull Island' provides an example of a third type of classic adventure: rescuing someone from a dangerous setting.

- Open the extract on the CD-ROM. Identify that the opening introduces an adventure story that is a journey. Explain that as only the opening has been written, the children can choose what happens next.

- Discuss the character Lord Edward. Who might he be? Ask for suggestions as to why he is keeping the note-writer captive. As the text is editable, change the villain to a character of the children's choosing, perhaps to a woman.

- Read through the note together. Ask: *Who would write a note like that?* Ask for suggestions. Perhaps it's a trick!

- Discuss what sort of place each location may be. Organise the children into groups, with each group taking one location and deciding what it is like. Again, if the class prefers, have fun changing the location – perhaps to a mountain or a city.

- Hand out copies of photocopiable page 15 'Skull Island map'. Ask the children to recreate the map as indicated and then to make notes around the map as to what might happen at each location.

- To establish the adventure story features in 'Skull Island', hand out photocopiable page 16 'Skull Island features' and ask the children to match each adventure feature to the relevant quotation from the story.

Poster: Adventure stories

What's on the CD-ROM

Adventure pointers
- Type in examples of the features used in *Jolly Roger* and *The Giant Postman*.

Adventure stories
- Roll over each adventure story feature to reveal examples from the extracts.

The 'Adventure stories' poster is a simple visual reminder of the basic elements of a sample adventure story. Display the poster during any sessions in which the children are writing adventure stories.

- Before displaying the poster, open 'Adventure pointers' on the CD-ROM. Remind the class of the adventure story features they have come across: heroes and scary characters, journeys and quests, action and suspense.

- Look back at the activity 'Skull Island features'. Explain to the children that they are going to carry out a similar activity now for the other two extracts. Ask them to find examples of the four features listed on the sign for each story, thinking about what might happen next and to type their thoughts in the boxes. This activity can also be carried out on photocopiable page 17.

- Now display the 'Adventure stories' poster on the CD-ROM and use it to consolidate the children's understanding of the adventure story features they have come across in the three text extracts. Roll over the features to reveal quotations from the extracts. Does this provide similar information to the children's answers to 'Adventure pointers' and the links that they made in 'Skull Island features'?

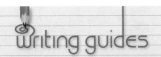

Extract 1: Jolly Roger

"That's it! I'll run away to sea and join the pirates and maybe I'll find my dad," thought Roger, getting excited. "And when I grow up and I'm all huge and hairy and covered in scars and my pockets are bulging with treasure, I'll come back and say 'Ha!' to my mum. 'Ha and fiddle-dee-dee! Take that! And that!'..."

While Roger was busy pretending to slice up his mum like a salami, he failed to notice (good job too, he would have had kittens!) a rowing boat sliding across the harbour towards him with an evil schloop, schloop, schloop. It was filled with such a pack of horrible, dirty, smelly, ugly, hairy, scary men as the world had ever seen. (Well, this part of the world anyway!) They oozed and slithered, as they had been taught at pirate school, out of the boat and up on to the quay.

Without so much as an " 'ow do y'do?" or an "excuse me", only " 'e'll do!", they stuffed – yes, stuffed – young Roger into a sack! Then they disappeared over the quayside into their boat and schloop-schlooped back to their ship, which was moored just outside the harbour mouth.

Roger struggled all the way like a ferret down a trouser leg.

From *Jolly Roger and the Pirates of Abdul the Skinhead*
by Colin McNaughton

Extract 2: The Giant Postman

BANG! BANG! BANG! Billy quickly opened the door and hid behind it.

"Here you are!" bellowed the Giant Postman and he dropped the parcel on to the floor. Then he stomped off down the street. THUMP! THUMP! THUMP!

"Has he gone?" whispered Billy's mum.

Billy peeped round the door.

"Yes, he's gone," he said.

Then Billy walked out into the street.

The street was still empty.

Mr White's garden gate was hanging off its hinges.

Mr Homer's cabbages were trampled to the ground.

Mrs Atwell's cat was on the roof of her house, quivering with fright.

One by one the villagers appeared. "Is it safe?" they asked.

"Yes," said Billy, "he's gone. But it's time we did something. Getting letters is supposed to be fun."

"We're all too scared to do anything," they said.

"Well, I'm not," said Billy. "I'm going to write the postman a letter and ask him to stop frightening us."

The crowd gasped.

"And I'm going to deliver it myself!"

From *The Giant Postman* by Sally Grindley

Text © 2000, Sally Grindley; illustration © 2000, Wendy Smith.

Extract 3: Skull Island

Kate watched the waves lapping against the rocks. It was a beautiful day.

That afternoon, her older cousin Shelly said she would take her out in the rowing boat. She looked across to Skull Island.

"That's the one place we won't be going," Shelly had said. "Lord Edward forbids anyone from landing there."

Just as Kate stood up to go she saw the bottle, bobbing in the waves, nearly hitting the rocks.

She let out a gasp of excitement and scuttled down the rocks to reach for it.

Inside she could see something she had only ever heard of in stories – a message in a bottle.

She uncorked it and shook it until the dry roll of paper fell into her hand. Unrolling it, she read the scrawled note:

Save me!!! I am a prisoner on Skull Island. I am being kept prisoner by Lord Edward, the wicked Lord of the Island. To reach my dungeon you need to land at the sandy beach, climb the steps of the secret tunnel, pass through the Outlaw's forest, cross the old rope bridge over Doom Ravine and climb Danger Mountain.

Kate bravely looked across the sea to the island. She was ready for adventure.

Illustrations © 2010, Martha Hardy.

Oh no!

● These events happened to Jolly Roger. Cut them out and put them in order.

A rowing boat got closer to Roger.
The pirates took Roger to their boat.
The pirates put Roger in the sack.
Roger said he would run away to sea.

Illustration © 2003, Martha Hardy.

What they thought

- Write down what each of the characters thought.

When the postman visited, Billy's mum thought:

When the postman left, the villagers thought:

When the postman had gone, Billy thought:

Illustration © 2000, Wendy Smith.

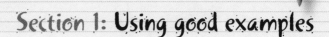
Skull Island map

● You have found the pieces of what looks like a map. Cut out these pieces and put them together on a separate sheet of paper to create a map of Skull Island.

● Make notes around your completed map to say what might happen at each location.

Illustrations © 2010, Martha Hardy.

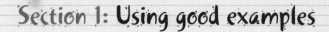
Skull Island features

● Draw lines to match up these adventure story features and quotations from 'Skull Island'.

A hero	Save me!!! I am a prisoner on Skull Island.
A quest	"That's the one place we won't be going," Shelly had said. "Lord Edward forbids anyone from landing there."
A scary character	To reach my dungeon you need to land at the sandy beach, climb the steps of the secret tunnel, pass through the Outlaw's forest, cross the old rope bridge over Doom Ravine and climb Danger Mountain.
A journey	Kate bravely looked across the sea to the island. She was ready for adventure.

Adventure pointers

● Can you find these four features in *Jolly Roger* and *The Giant Postman*? Write them in the spaces by the sign.

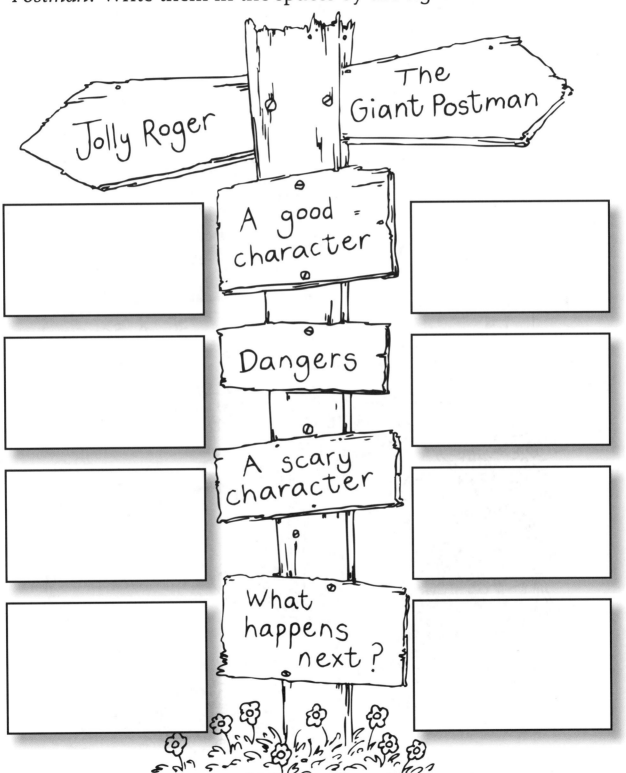

Illustration © 2003, Martha Hardy.

Adventure stories

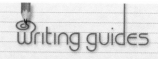

Section 2
Developing writing

The activities in this section allow children to focus on individual features of adventure stories, encouraging them to gain confidence and build up a bank of ideas for use when they create their own adventure story. You might choose to undertake these activities alongside planning a piece of writing or, alternatively, you could use them as one-off creative sessions.

Creating a hero

The first two activities in this section help the children to develop a hero for their adventure story, and to think about what he or she can do. Keep this simple! Don't burden your Bat-belt with all sorts of gadgets and abilities. The children may also want to consider their hero having an Achilles heel, to increase the tension in an adventure story, such as Indiana Jones with his snakes or Superman with his Kryptonite. Every hero should have some flaw that has the potential to bring them down. There is a dynamic interaction in adventure stories between characters and the dangers they face, which is why children could think of their hero in relation to the various challenges set in the story.

Another two activities covered in this section ('Meetings' and in particular 'Create a villain') provide a frame for the children to think about the 'bad guys' in their story. In many adventure stories the villains are the most interesting character and the most fun to write.

On a journey

An adventure story takes the form of an extended plot, in which there are various dangers along the route towards the hero's goal. The activities 'Journey to the unknown' and 'Quest devising' help the children to tackle writing about this type of episodic quest, with dangers along the way. What's vital here is the way an adventure story extends the middle section of writing. If everything is solved in the first paragraph, where's the adventure? Stories need movement through a series of risks and dangers: the journey their character will make, and the villains and dangers they will encounter along the way.

Adventure language

The activities 'Adventure words' and 'It's all in the detail' scaffold the children's use of adventure language, focusing on adventurous vocabulary to enhance the sentences they write in their stories. An adventure story is nothing without atmosphere – these activities will help the children to develop their language skills in this way.

Activities breakdown

Character
- It's hero time (page 20)
- Meetings (page 21)
- Create a villain (page 22)

Plot
- Survivor (page 20)
- Journey to the unknown (page 21)
- Quest devising (page 24)

Setting
- Heroes and heroines at work (page 22)
- Your senses of adventure (page 24)

Language
- Adventure words (page 23)
- It's all in the detail (page 23)

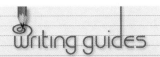

Activity 1: It's hero time

Objective

To use key features of narrative in their own writing. (Year 1 Strand 9)

What's on the CD-ROM

It's hero time
- Type in details to create an adventure hero.

What to do

In this activity, the children create their own adventure story hero.

- Recap the types of plot that adventure stories have – a series of disasters or problems to solve on a journey before achieving a final goal. Ask: *Who might be able to overcome these problems?* The heroes in the extracts in Section 1 have no particular heroic qualities except bravery. Other heroes might have 'normal' attributes, such as being clever or strong, or they might have magical or superhuman powers, such as being able to fly or X-ray vision. Talk about the attributes of heroes in other adventure stories the children have encountered.

- Open 'It's hero time' on the CD-ROM. Brainstorm lists of attributes, catchphrases and gadgets that a hero or heroine might use. Try to get a good mix of real and superhuman attributes. Create a model character as a class. Ask: *Is our hero going to have superhuman powers? What clever things will the character say? What gadget or useful equipment will he or she carry?* Save the class notes for use in the next activity.

- Hand out copies of photocopiable page 25 'It's hero time' and ask the children to create a hero character of their own devising.

Activity 2: Survivor

Objective

To use planning to establish clear sections for writing. (Year 2 Strand 10)

What's on the CD-ROM

It's hero time
- Recap the hero character created.

Media resources
- Use the audio clip as stimulus for discussion.

Survivor
- Drag and drop options to help the hero escape.
- Type in your own action for the hero.

What to do

In this activity children explore how their hero responds to danger.

- Open the saved version of the CD-ROM activity 'It's hero time' and recap on the attributes of the newly created character.

- Next, ask the children to suggest a disaster that might happen to this character (for example, being kidnapped by pirates). Ask: *How might the hero use their attributes and gadgets to escape? What might they say to the pirates?* Model writing a couple of sentences about this.

- Play the audio clip on the CD-ROM. Ask: *What dangers does this sound conjure up? In what way does the sound do this? How will the hero overcome this peril?* Read out the following dangerous event and play the audio clip again: *There was a rumble then the earth shook.*

- Open 'Survivor' on the CD-ROM. Ask the children to choose from the options provided in each scenario and drag and drop the action that the hero might take in each case. There is also space for the children to type in other possible actions that the hero might take.

- Finally, provide each child with a copy of photocopiable page 26 'Survivor'. Ensure they also have their completed copies of photocopiable page 25 'It's hero time'. Ask them to write sentences describing what their character might do in order to survive each scenario (preferably different actions from those in the whole-class activity). Encourage the children to remain true to the character that they have created.

 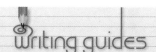

Activity 3: Journey to the unknown

Objective

To sustain form in narrative, including use of person and time.
(Year 2 Strand 9)

What's on the CD-ROM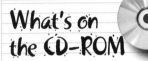

Media resources
- Display the four images and discuss what dangers lurk in each setting.

Journey to the unknown
- Drag and drop three settings to create a journey.
- Type brief descriptions of what will happen to the hero in each setting.

What to do

In this activity children create a dangerous journey for their hero.

- Display the four images provided on the CD-ROM. Discuss what dangers may lurk in each setting.

- Re-cap on the importance of journeys through dangerous settings in adventure stories. Remind the children that each of the three extracts in Section 1 requires the main character to go on a journey to save the day.

- Display 'Journey to the unknown' on the CD-ROM. Explain that the class hero has to go on a quest. With the children, choose three of the locations from the 'Image bank' for the hero's journey. Ask for suggestions about what happens to the hero in each setting and type in their ideas.

- Organise the children to work in small groups. Allow time for the groups to carry out the activity to choose their own adventure journey, either on screen or using photocopiable page 27, where they can cut out the settings of their choosing to include in the journey.

- Encourage the children to write a couple of sentences about each picture. Ask: *What danger does the hero encounter at each setting? How might he or she overcome it?* Invite the children to write a sentence before the first picture and after the third picture to create a beginning and an end for their story.

Activity 4: Meetings

Objective

To draw on knowledge and experience of texts in deciding and planning what and how to write.
(Year 2 Strand 9)

What to do

In this activity children introduce a villain to their story.

- Discuss the villains and dangers encountered in the three text extracts (pages 10–12): the pirates, the Giant Postman and Lord Edward.

- Choose a problem character from photocopiable page 28 'Meetings' and ask for suggestions from the class about the character: *What are they like? Are they evil? If so, why? What might they say and do to the hero?* Write the children's ideas on the board, then model writing a scene in which the class hero encounters this villain.

- Organise the children into groups. Give each group photocopiable page 28. Ask the children to cut out the cards and lay them face down on the table. They should take turns to choose a card and to describe their villain to the group. What would happen if their hero or heroine met this character?

- Once each child has chosen a villain, ask them to work independently to write the scene in which this meeting takes place. More confident children could write further scenes featuring different villains.

Activity 5: Create a villain

Objective

To make adventurous word and language choices appropriate to the style and purpose of the text. (Year 2 Strand 9)

What's on the CD-ROM

Create a villain
- Roll over questions to reveal prompts.
- Type in details to create a villainous character.

What to do
In this activity the children will invent a truly horrible villain for their adventure story.

- Open 'Create a villain' on the CD-ROM. Explain to the children that together you are going to create the vilest, meanest, strangest, cruellest villain you can collectively come up with.

- Go back to the extract 'Jolly Roger' on the CD-ROM and circle the words that show how foul the pirates are: they are horrid to look at, to smell, and probably to touch. They even move in a horrid way. Talk about some of the villains that the children know from books they have read or programmes they have watched on TV. Develop the children's discussion about these characters and capture any appropriate adjectives and aspects.

- Now return to 'Create a villain' on the CD-ROM. Use some of the suggested words and attributes in the roll over text, along with any other ideas from the children, to type in villainous details and create a nasty character.

- Organise the children to either work on screen or use photocopiable page 29 'Create a villain' to create their own villain.

Activity 6: Heroes and heroines at work

Objective

To visualise and comment on events, characters and ideas, making imaginative links to their own experiences. (Year 1 Strand 8)

What's on the CD-ROM

Media resources
- Display the four images and use effective language to describe them.
- Play the audio clip to create a sense of atmosphere.

What to do
In this activity the children are encouraged to describe settings with atmosphere.

- Display the four images from the CD-ROM. Choose one to focus on (for example, the 'Desert island'). With the children, brainstorm words they might use to describe the island to make it sound more exciting, such as 'a wild, dangerous, jungly, haunted island' and so on. While you are doing this, you might like to play the audio clip to stimulate the children's thinking about these scenarios.

- Now provide each child with a copy of photocopiable page 30 'Heroes and heroines at work'. Invite them to look at each of the pictures with a partner and share anything they notice about each scene. Encourage them to choose one of the pictures, cut it out and stick it onto the middle of a large piece of paper. Challenge them to find three dangers in the scene and to write a sentence about each around the image. Encourage them to think of a suitable adjective (such as 'angry' or 'cunning') for a pirate.

- As an extension activity, ask the children to draw and describe their own setting, such as, a jungle, a city or a big, old house. Ensure that they fill it with plenty of atmospheric detail.

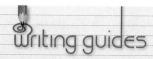

Activity 7: Adventure words

Objective

To make adventurous word and language choices appropriate to the style and purpose of the text. (Year 2 Strand 9)

What to do
The children will practise using a range of prepositions to describe how the hero gets around, under and over various obstacles.

- Remind the children that adventure stories often include many obstacles that the main character must negotiate on their journey. Can the children suggest any ways of getting around an obstacle? Make a note of their ideas on the board, for example, 'around', 'over', 'under' and so on. Model using these words to create sentences for an adventure story, such as 'The pirate squeezed under the drawbridge'.

- Take a couple of the prepositions on photocopiable page 31 'Adventure words' ('through', 'into', 'under', 'over', 'up', 'down') and write them on the board. As a piece of shared writing, write one sentence for each preposition, varying the scenarios as much as possible.

- Hand out photocopiable page 31 'Adventure words'. Ask the children to write one sentence in each box using the word given. Can they use a different character, verb and setting or obstacle for each sentence? For example: 'I crawled through the dark woods.' 'He ran into the bear cage.'

- The children might be inspired by their earlier work on photocopiable pages 26, 27 or 30, or the four images available on the CD-ROM.

Activity 8: It's all in the detail

Objective

To make adventurous word and language choices appropriate to the style and purpose of the text. (Year 2 Strand 9)

What's on the CD-ROM

It's all in the detail
- Drag arrows to match simple sentences with more exciting versions.

Media resources
- Play the audio clip to create a sense of atmosphere.

What to do
In this activity children are challenged to improve simple adventure story sentences by adding detail.

- Write a simple sentence on the board, such as 'I fought the pirate'. Show how to embellish this to make it more dramatic. ('Barehanded, I fought the wild, bloodthirsty pirate on the wobbly gangplank.')

- Open 'It's all in the detail' on the CD-ROM and invite the children to match up each simple sentence with its exciting counterpart. This can be done in pairs or as a class. Talk to the children about how the expanded sentences have improved the original simple versions.

- Hand out photocopiable page 32 'It's all in the detail'. Ask the children to take each sentence in turn and write a longer, more interesting version below it. For example: 'I was excited because I found a golden envelope.' 'I quickly made a long ladder out of the branches.' 'We saw a fearsome dinosaur lunging towards us.'

- While the children are carrying out this activity, play the audio clip on the CD-ROM to create a sense of atmosphere.

- At the end of the activity, share the children's sentences. Who has created the longest sentence? Who has created the most exciting?

Activity 9: Your senses of adventure

Objective

To visualise and comment on events, characters and ideas, making imaginative links to their own experiences.
(Year 1 Strand 8)

What's on the CD-ROM

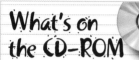

Media resources
- Use the four images to stimulate the children's imagination.

What to do

In this activity the children put themselves in an adventure setting and imagine what their senses tell them about their immediate environment.

- Display the four images from the 'Media resources' section of the CD-ROM. Choose one image setting to work on (for example, 'Rope bridge'). Ask the children to close their eyes and imagine that they are on the bridge. Ask: *What do you hear?* Capture any ideas, making notes around the image using the annotation tools. Develop their ideas if appropriate: perhaps they can hear water below them, the bridge breaking, animals nearby, the sound of pursuers. If you are able to provide some sound effects yourself then have fun doing that.

- Now ask: *What can you see? What can you feel? What can you smell? How do you feel? What do you say?* Capture the children's answers at each stage.

- Hand out photocopiable page 33 'Your senses of adventure' to pairs of children. Ask one child to pretend they are in one of the other three image settings and get their partner to ask them the questions on the sheet and to make notes. Challenge the children to get a 'yuk' or 'help' out of their partner. Allow time for both children in each pair to carry out the activity.

Activity 10: Quest devising

Objective

To use key features of narrative in their own writing. (Year 1 Strand 9)

What to do

In this activity the children are provided with features of a quest adventure to choose from to create a simple story plan.

- Remind the children of the three text extracts in Section 1 (pages 10–12). Each of these ends with the possibility of a quest: in *Jolly Roger*, there is a suggestion that Roger will go and find his father; in *The Giant Postman*, Billy prepares to visit the Giant Postman; *Skull Island* sets up the scene for Kate to go and rescue the message writer.

- Provide each child with photocopiable page 34 'Quest devising'. Explain to the children that their challenge is to create exciting scenarios for at least six of the quest set-ups on the photocopiable sheet. Model choosing scenarios for the first couple. For example: 'The hero wants to **find** his way back home.' 'The hero wants to **get away from** the monster in the underwater cave.'

- Once the children have filled in at least six of the scenario starters on the sheet, ask them to choose one or two of the quest features to create a very simple adventure quest plan.

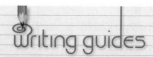

It's hero time

● Your adventure story needs a hero. Create this character below.

Draw your hero here

Name: _____

Special abilities: _____

_____

_____

Catchphrase: _____

_____

Special equipment: _____

_____

_____

Survivor

- Watch out – here are some dangers!
- What would your hero do in each of these situations?

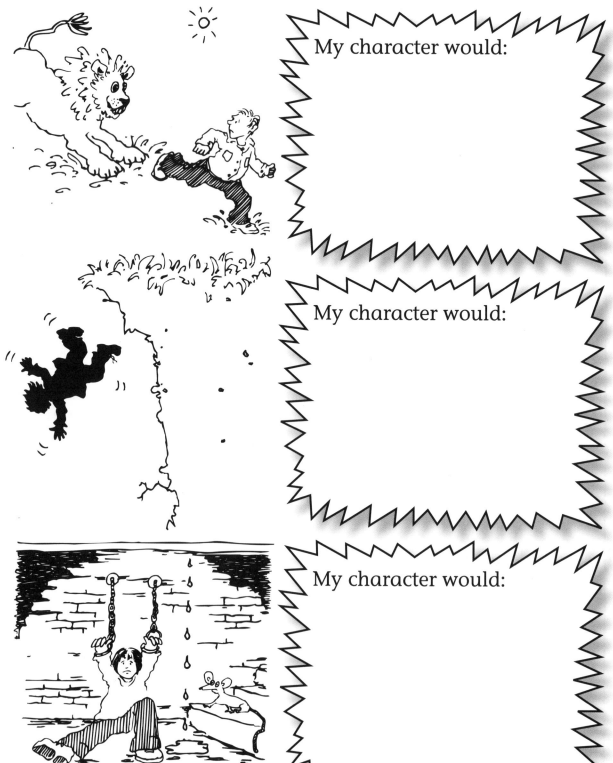

My character would:

My character would:

My character would:

Illustrations © 2003, Martha Hardy.

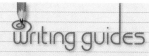

Journey to the unknown

- Here are some places you could use for your hero's journey.
- Cut them out, choose three places and decide what will happen in each.

a dark cave

a tall tower

a big ship

an old bridge

a deep passage

a high balloon

a speeding bus

a foaming river

a steep mountain

Illustrations © 2003, Martha Hardy.

Meetings

● Which villains might your hero meet on their adventure?
Cut out the cards, select one and then describe the villain.

pirate

burglar

dinosaur

giant bird

crazy inventor

one-eyed giant monster

Illustrations © 2003, Martha Hardy.

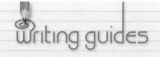

Photocopiable

Create a villain

● Fill in the character card to devise a really nasty villain for your adventure story.

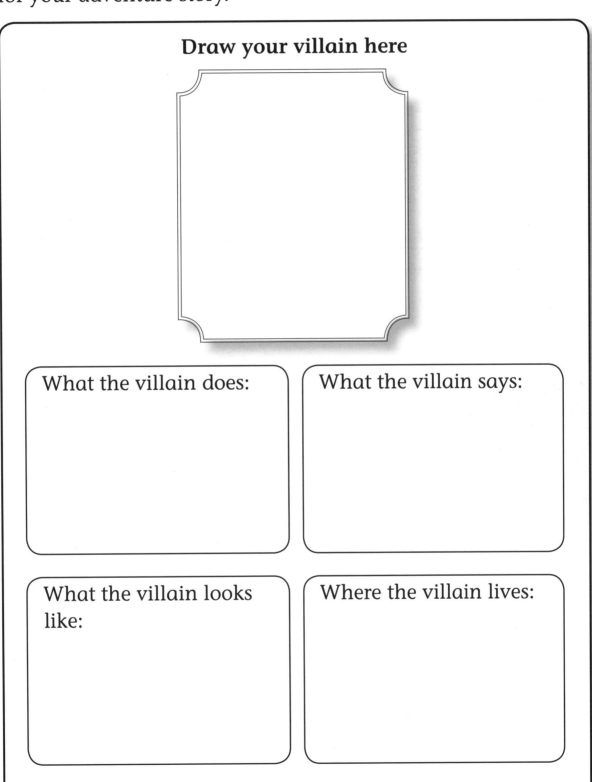

Draw your villain here

What the villain does:

What the villain says:

What the villain looks like:

Where the villain lives:

Photocopiable **SCHOLASTIC** www.scholastic.co.uk

Heroes and heroines at work

● On another sheet write about the dangers in each setting.

Adventure words

● Use these words to write some sentences for your adventure story. Try to make each sentence different.

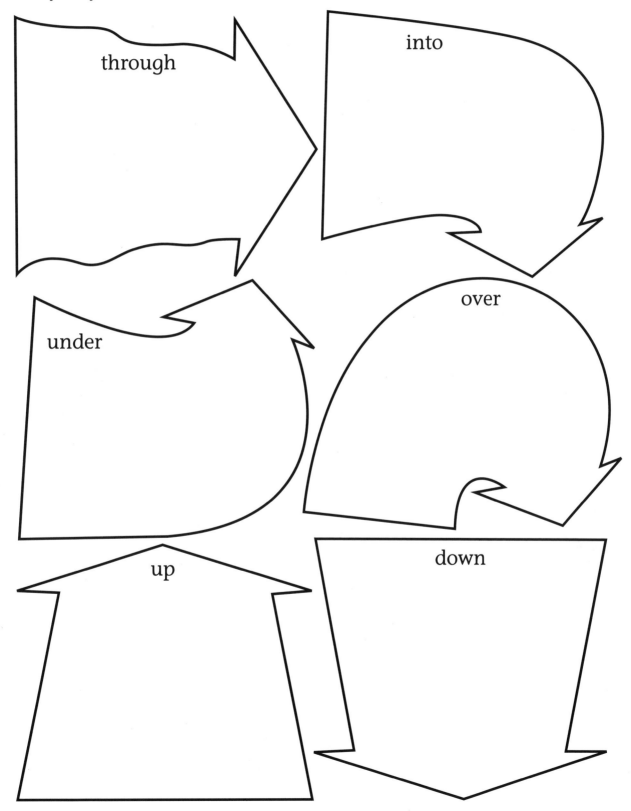

It's all in the detail

● Make these sentences more exciting.

I found an envelope.

_____

_____

I made a ladder.

_____

_____

We saw a dinosaur.

_____

_____

A bird flew past.

_____

_____

The door opened.

_____

_____

Illustrations © 2003, Martha Hardy.

writing guides

Your senses of adventure

● Close your eyes and pretend you are in one of the four image settings your teacher has shown you. Ask your partner the following questions and write down their answers:

What can you see?	What can you hear?
What do you touch and how does it feel?	What does it smell like?
What do you say about this place?	How do you feel about it?

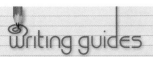

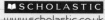
Quest devising

● Fill in six of the following quest features. Then choose two of your favourite to put in your story plan.

Your hero wants to:

find...	get away from...
explore...	capture...
reach...	help...
save...	escape from...
meet...	beat...
solve...	discover...

Section 3

Writing

A sense of adventure – this old phrase sums up what we need to develop in our young writers, inspiring them to take the ideas of previous sections and turn them into an extended story. This section prepares the children to write their own extended adventure story. In Sections 1 and 2 of this book, they have investigated heroes, journeys and dangers in the form of scary/nasty characters and settings, and will have some of these elements to use in their story. Now it's time to build the elements into an adventure story. The activities covered in this section provide children with support at a range of levels. 'Adventure pick and mix' provides greater support than 'Adventure Island' – this might support differentiation or a gradual 'easing in' to story writing. The template on photocopiable pages 42–43 'Adventure kit' is a planning grid that the children can use to help them plan any adventure story they are aiming to write. This planning frame is designed to ensure that the children include in their writing all the key elements required to make a successful adventure story.

Using the 'My adventure story' template

The 'My adventure story' section on the CD-ROM provides a framework for the children to create a 'designed' story. It's worth spending time familiarising yourself with the writing templates before modelling how to use them with the children.

When 'My adventure story' is open on the CD-ROM, you will be able to choose from one of six layouts for a page. The layouts have text boxes (which give you the opportunity to change the size of the font) as well as image boxes. All the images in the book have been provided in the 'Image bank' and can be dragged into the image boxes. New images can also be uploaded into the 'Image bank' so that the children can select and draw specific images for their story. (For more information about uploading the children's own images please refer to the 'Help file'.) Speech and thought bubbles can also be added to the illustrations.

Once an adventure story is complete, there is the option to create a book cover. Open 'Cover' from the main menu of the CD-ROM. This cover template will allow you to add titles, images, logos, barcodes, blurb and a price.

Each story can be saved on your system. It's worth organising a saving protocol so that the children can easily save and re-access their work.

Writing tips

- Give the adventure a clear goal – what does the hero need to do?
- Create a few dangers that make the goal difficult.
- Have a nasty villain.
- Spend time on a danger, describing what it was like and how it felt.
- Keep your reader wondering whether the hero will make it through the dangers.

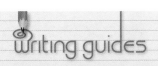

Project 1: Adventure pick and mix

Objective

To use planning to establish clear sections for writing. (Year 2 Strand 10)

What's on the CD-ROM

Adventure pick and mix
- Roll over the adventure story elements to reveal question prompts to refine the children's thinking.

Adventure kit
- Complete the story planning frame.

My adventure story
- Compose a story using the writing templates.

What to do

This project provides a selection of adventure story elements that can be combined to create the skeleton of an adventure story.

- Open 'Adventure pick and mix' on the CD-ROM. This activity provides a 'mix and match' selection of incidents that might occur in an adventure story. Display the first screen showing the opening options. Roll over each option to reveal questions designed to stimulate children's ideas. Discuss the possible answers with the children. Repeat with the story middles and the story endings.

- Cut out the cards from photocopiable pages 38–39 'Adventure pick and mix'. Give groups of three children one beginning, two middles and an ending for their story.

- Ensure the CD-ROM version of this activity is available so that the children can remind themselves of the prompt questions. Encourage the groups to discuss each scenario in turn, thinking of possible answers to the questions on each card and on screen, to create scenes for an adventure story.

- After the discussion, encourage the children to work independently as they plan and then write their own version of the story.

- To help the children plan their story, hand out photocopiable pages 42–43 'Adventure kit' or, if possible, make it available on screen for the children to type in notes.

- When the children are ready to start writing, display the 'My adventure story' writing templates and explain to the children how to use them. Model how they can choose one of the six layouts for each new page of their story. Discuss when each template might be most appropriate.

- Open the 'Cover' template and model how to complete it. Point out the space for the blurb and price, as well as the publisher's name.

- Provide time for the children to write their stories in this way. Don't forget to organise a filing protocol so that everyone can easily re-access their story and no one makes the mistake of saving over someone else's version.

- Depending on the time and number of computers available, the children could write on blank templates that you have printed out. You could also print out the stories before they are illustrated and let the children illustrate them by hand. It is also possible to upload the children's own images into the 'Image bank' for use in their stories.

Project 2: Adventure Island

What to do
This project provides inspiration for the children to write an adventure story similar to the *Skull Island* starter in Section 1.

● Give small groups of children photocopiable pages 40–41, 'Adventure Island'. Look at the note and ask: *What questions does the note raise?* (For example: *Why might someone go after the treasure? What sort of treasure is it going to be?*) Tell the children to write down their ideas.

● Invite the children to look at the map of Adventure Island on photocopiable page 40. Encourage them to pick out the details (a tunnel through the mountain and a rope bridge across the ravine) and to suggest what could happen at each location.

● Next, ask the children to decode the first secret message (it reads: 'It's in the tower'). Are they beginning to see how the story might progress? Decode the second note (it reads: 'Beware of the pirates'). Ask the children to think about the equipment their hero has with them. They also need to plan how they will outwit and defeat the pirates.

● Let the children use their ideas to plan a first-person adventure story telling how they found the treasure.

● The children may use 'Adventure kit' on the CD-ROM or photocopiable pages 42–43 to assist them in ordering their thoughts.

● Encourage them to use the 'My adventure story' templates to create their final versions.

Project 3: Bags of adventure

What to do
This project aims to stimulate the children's imagination for adventure.

● Before the lesson gather various items to place in a bag. The items will be used to inspire plots and themes in an adventure story. For example, the item could initiate a quest (something to find) or the item could inspire a theme or setting (an alien toy could suggest a space adventure). Try to ensure the objects interest both girls and boys. Possible items you could collect are: a necklace, padlock, torch, peg doll, plastic spider, alien toy, jigsaw pieces, mask, perfume bottle, mirror and shoe.

● At the beginning of the lesson ask each child to pick one or more objects from the bag and to use them as the basis of an adventure story.

● To help the children with planning, open 'Adventure kit' on the CD-ROM and recap the features they need to include. Then supply photocopiable pages 42–43 'Adventure kit' for them to plan their story individually.

● Finally, invite the children to write their story using the 'My adventure story' writing templates on the CD-ROM.

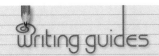

Adventure pick and mix

● Select adventure story elements to include in your own story.

Beginnings	Middles

We found a treasure map.

What did the map show?

A trapdoor opened.

Where was the trapdoor?

We went to the castle.

What did we find
in the castle?

We were trapped in a cave.

What was the cave like?

We had to find our lost dog.

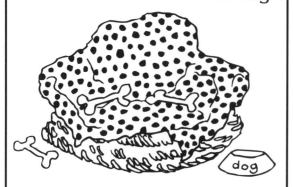

Why was the dog lost?

We found a rickety bridge.

How could we cross
the bridge?

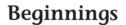
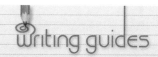

Illustrations © 2003, Martha Hardy.

Middles

We found a key.

What did it open?

There was a rope swing.

What was it over?

There was a crocodile in our way.

How did we get past the crocodile?

Endings

We escaped from the villain.

Who was the villain?

We found the treasure.

Where did we find it?

We found the dog.

Where did we find him?

Adventure Island

● Plan an adventure that takes place on this island.

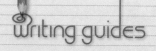

● Use these details to help your hero.

Message found in an old library

The treasure of Old Ben Mieleniewski is hidden on Adventure Island.

Other papers you found

rg'h rm
gsv gldvi

yvdziv
lu gsv
krizgvh

Top secret code book

Code

a	= z		n	= m
b	= y		o	= l
c	= x		p	= k
d	= w		q	= j
e	= v		r	= i
f	= u		s	= h
g	= t		t	= g
h	= s		u	= f
i	= r		v	= e
j	= q		w	= d
k	= p		x	= c
l	= o		y	= b
m	= n		z	= a

Equipment

torch

rope ladder

map

sandwiches

drink

compass

binoculars

camera

Illustrations © 2003, Martha Hardy.

Adventure kit

● Use this kit to plan your adventure story.

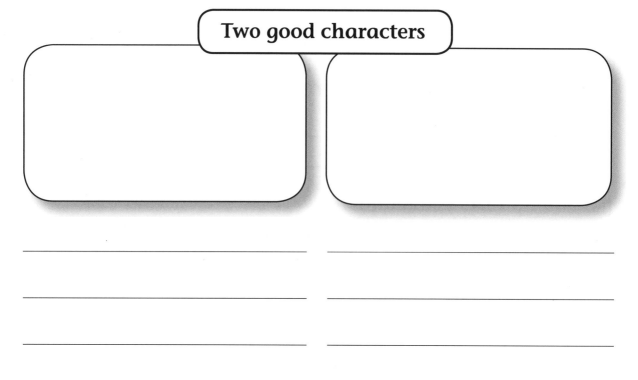

Two good characters

_____

_____

_____

A scary character

_____

_____

_____

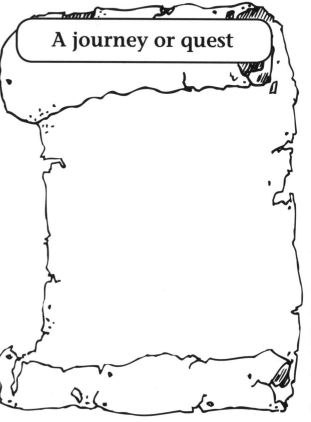

A journey or quest

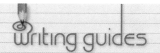

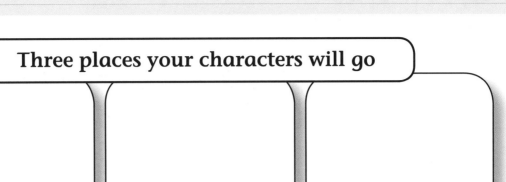

Three places your characters will go

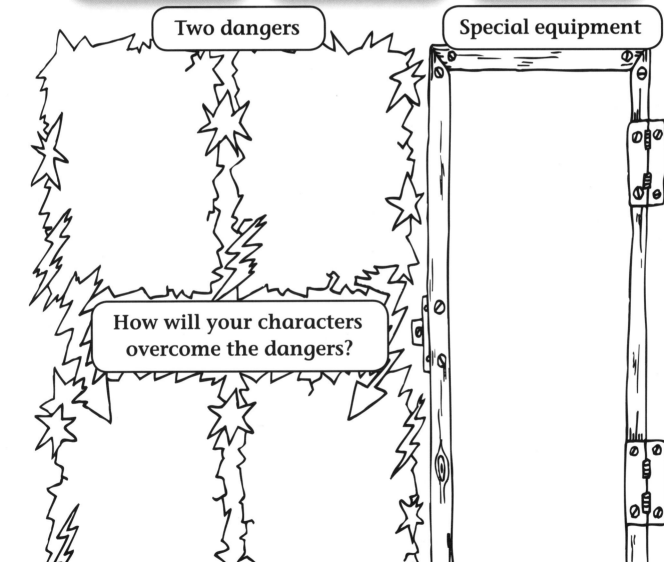

Two dangers

Special equipment

How will your characters overcome the dangers?

Illustrations © 2003, Martha Hardy.

Review

Encourage the children to review their progress during and after writing. The photocopiables in this section support self, peer and teacher review.

Self review

Hand out photocopiable page 45 'Self review' and invite the children to examine their own stories by choosing three parts that could be improved. For example, imagine the main character is swinging on a rope. To add tension a writer could:

● make the situation more exciting or dangerous (the rope could be breaking)

● describe the situation in a more exciting way (the writer could add more descriptive words about the rope and what lies beneath it)

● explain how the character feels – are they scared and worried?

Peer review

Explain to the children that the first step in evaluating a piece of writing is to select the parts of the story that work well. Invite them to read their partner's story and underline the best bits. Then hand out photocopiable page 46 'Peer review' for the children to complete.

Invite the children to discuss their answers with their partner. Can they explain why a particular character is their favourite, or why they liked a particular part of the plot?

Teacher review

The assessment chart provides a focus on activities in Section 2 and 3. This genre of writing lends itself to developing certain writing skills that can provide a focus for assessment. Photocopiable page 47 provides the main ones – though it should be used in conjunction with APP materials.

● At sentence level the main focus should be on using the past tense to recount the events of the story, though children may occasionally use the present tense to vividly present an adventure moment ('He jumps off the train.').

● Variation of sentences may emerge naturally – for example, starters such as 'Suddenly...' lend themselves to adventurous moments.

● A significant focus lies in AF4 and AF1. The adventure goal provides the shape of the story.

● The relevance and appropriate choices of subject matter will be evident in children keeping to their adventure's goals and dangers.

● Appropriate word choice can be developed as children select the nouns that would feature in such a story and modify them with appropriate adjectives, such as a bridge becoming a 'rickety bridge'.

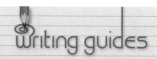

Self review

● How could you make your story better? Fill in the boxes.

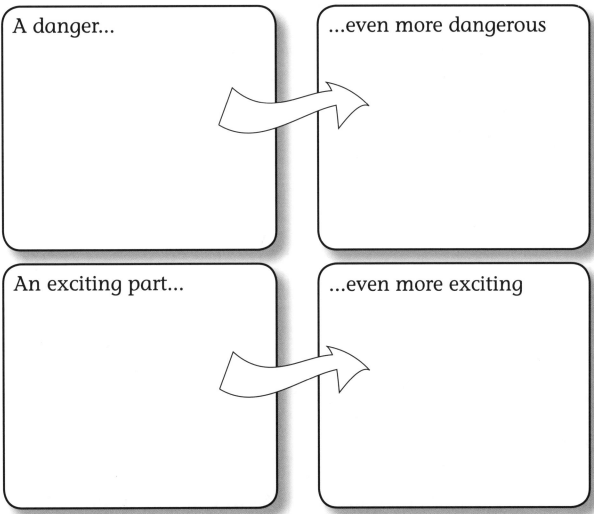

A danger...

...even more dangerous

An exciting part...

...even more exciting

● Now choose your own part of the story and make it even better.

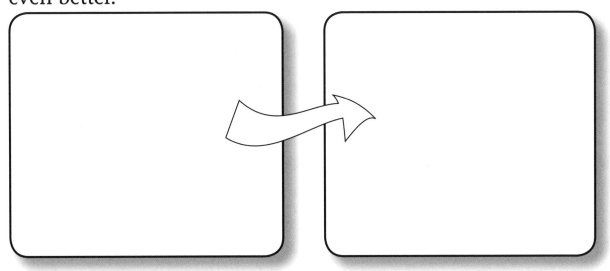

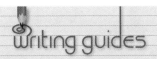

Photocopiable ■SCHOLASTIC www.scholastic.co.uk

Peer review

- Read your partner's adventure story. Give awards to your favourite parts of the story.

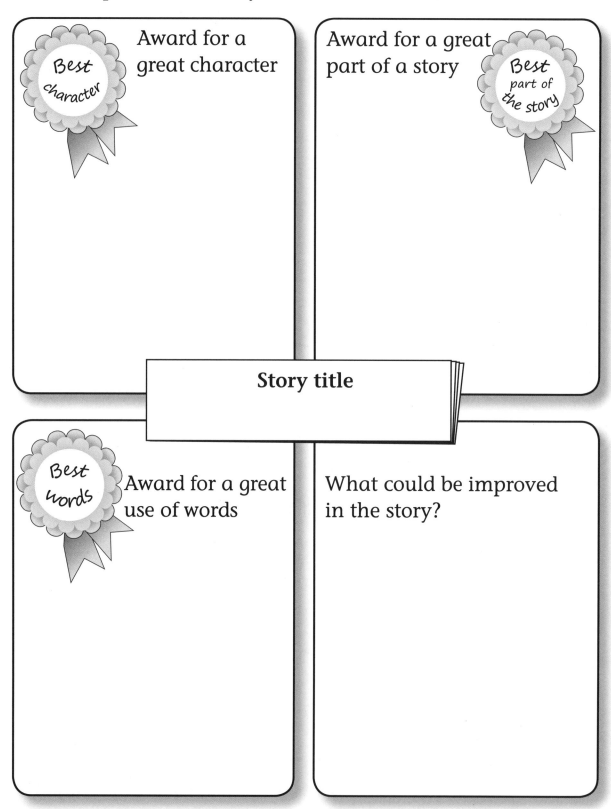

Best character

Award for a great character

Award for a great part of a story

Best part of the story

Story title

Best words

Award for a great use of words

What could be improved in the story?

Teacher review

	AF5 Vary sentences for clarity, purpose and effect.	AF6 Write with technical accuracy of syntax and punctuation in phrases, clauses and sentences.	AF3 Organise and present whole texts effectively, sequencing and structuring information, ideas and events.	AF4 Construct paragraphs and use cohesion within and between paragraphs.	AF1 Write imaginative, interesting and thoughtful texts.	AF2 Produce texts which are appropriate to task, reader and purpose.	AF7 Select appropriate and effective vocabulary.
LEVEL 1	Simple retelling of adventurous events.	Mostly grammatically accurate clauses. Some awareness of use of full stops and capital letters *e.g. beginning/end of sentence.*	Events/ideas sometimes in appropriate order. Some formulaic phrases indicate start/end of text, *e.g. 'Once upon a time', 'One day', 'The end'.*	Simple connections between ideas, events, *i.e. one event follows another.*	Simple adventure events conveyed through appropriate word choice. Some descriptive language, *e.g. 'scary forest'.*	Some indication of basic story form, with a purpose to the adventure.	Mostly simple vocabulary that communicates features of an adventure story.
LEVEL 2	Consistent use of past tense. Some variation, with exciting ideas such as sentences that start with adverbs *e.g. 'Suddenly...'.*	Clause structure is mostly grammatically correct. Sentence demarcation with capital letters and full stops usually accurate.	Use of adventure pattern to sequence events, using time-related words or phrases. Adventure planning begins to show in the organisation of narrative.	Ideas in sections grouped by content, some linking by temporal markers *e.g. 'Next...', 'After that...'.*	Mostly relevant ideas and content – events that contain elements of adventure. Some apt word choices to create interest, notably in description. Character's viewpoint may be communicated in thoughts and feelings.	Main features of story planning demonstrate sense of purpose. Some attempts to adopt appropriate style.	Simple, often speech-like vocabulary conveys relevant meanings. Some adventurous word choices.

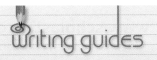

■SCHOLASTIC

Also available in this series:

ISBN 978-1407-11253-4

ISBN 978-1407-11265-7

ISBN 978-1407-11267-1

ISBN 978-1407-11256-5

ISBN 978-1407-11270-1

ISBN 978-1407-11248-0

ISBN 978-1407-11254-1

ISBN 978-1407-11266-4

ISBN 978-1407-11258-9

ISBN 978-1407-11268-8

ISBN 978-1407-11251-0

ISBN 978-1407-11257-2

ISBN 978-1407-11255-8

ISBN 978-1407-11269-5

ISBN 978-1407-11250-3

ISBN 978-1407-11247-3

ISBN 978-1407-11252-7

ISBN 978-1407-11264-0

ISBN 978-1407-11249-7

ISBN 978-1407-11260-2

ISBN 978-1407-11261-9

ISBN 978-1407-11263-3

ISBN 978-1407-11259-6

ISBN 978-1407-11262-6

To find out more, call: **0845 603 9091** or visit our website: **www.scholastic.co.uk**